TRUE PARANORMAL EXPERIENCES

Shirley Crowe

Order this book online at www.trafford.com
or email orders@trafford.com

Most Trafford titles are also available at major online book retailers.

Printed in the United States of America.

ISBN: 978-1-4669-1149-9 (sc)
ISBN: 978-1-4669-1150-5 (e)

Trafford rev. 01/13/2012

 www.trafford.com

North America & international
toll-free: 1 888 232 4444 (USA & Canada)
phone: 250 383 6864 ♦ fax: 812 355 4082

DEDICATION

This book is dedicated to my husband and daughter, with love and admiration. I never would have finished it without their love and encouragement. I dearly love them both!

---❖---

CONTENTS

Dedication v

Prologue.. ix

About the Author.. xi

Acknowledgments xiii

The House the Ghost Built and Dwelled In........................... 1

The Frankenstein Monster... 6

The Slamming Doors 8

The Dismembered Arm 10

A Burglar? I Think Not. 11

The Peeping Spirit 12

Wrestling with the Middletown Cemetery Ghost 13

The Goose-Stepping Ghost.. 15

The Cemetery Dare 16

Follow the Sound of the Footsteps....................................... 18

"A Restless Soul".. 20

A Man with No Face 21

PROLOGUE

This book contains true-life experiences of every imaginable kind. Sit back in your seat and hold on tight, because these tales weren't written in an attempt to get your attention; indeed, these truly did happen.

Ghosts have been a large part of my life since childhood. I have had numerous encounters with all sorts of fascinating things—so many, in fact, that it would wear out my fingers to put them all in writing. These encounters are not limited only to spirits; I have also known things will happen before they occur. In my mind's eye, I can see an event taking place before it happens, even if it is as simple as an unannounced call or visit. Simply put, I was born with ESP, extrasensory perception. I believe this sixth sense has increased my ability to tune in to wavelengths of every kind of spirit.

Some people never experience a sighting of anything spookier than a Halloween mask or a scary movie, but there are many places—registered haunted houses, homes, and hotels—that provide an opportunity to open one's eyes to another time and place. If you are interested in a haunted, eight-room house with three bedrooms and one small bath, located in a valley in Ohio, then I know just the right place for you.

Sweet dreams!

---◆---

ABOUT THE AUTHOR

Shirley Crowe was born in Middleton, Ohio. She loves nature and animals. She is descended from Scottish, Welsh, and Cherokee Indian bloodlines. She has one daughter who is a blessing, an answer to a prayer. Shirley is married to a wonderful man, Buddy, and together they reside in a little town outside of Huntsville, Alabama. Shirley moved there to be close to "her girl."

❖

ACKNOWLEDGMENTS

Special thanks to Gwyn Wright for her greatly needed help in putting this book together.

THE HOUSE THE GHOST BUILT AND DWELLED IN

The events in this story occurred when I was in my preteen years. We lived in an older home, which was entirely built by a Greek family (whose name I will withhold for obvious reasons). But we didn't buy this particular home from the original owners, the Greeks; we bought it from an American family (whose name I will withhold to protect the innocent, namely me). So we knew nothing about the family that built the home until many years later.

Since this man was said to be well-to-do, this house was built with the best materials. After living in the house for a short time and being told by the previous owner that this house was haunted, we dismissed the stories and resumed our normal activities.

The house was in a small town in Ohio. It was a two-story home with three bedrooms and one bathroom. At the start, ten people lived in this house. Soon after, my mother's mother moved in because of her debilitating arthritis. My only child was born, and then the fun began. In the bathroom, my brother heard and felt heavy breathing on the nape of his neck. He was shaving at the time and saw no reflection in the mirror. Turning, he saw nothing standing anywhere near him. He finished shaving and came downstairs, telling the tale to family members there and saying it didn't scare him.

My other brother was in the bathroom, washing his face and preparing to shave, when a towel hanging close on the wall began to sway, slowly at first, and then faster and faster. He got goosebumps on that occasion and told us so.

Mom and I were on the front porch, talking and drinking coffee, when a neighbor next door stepped onto her porch. She noticed us chatting and called for Mom's attention. After a very short chat, the neighbor informed Mom that the house we lived in was registered as haunted.

Mom replied, "You're a little late with that news. We were already informed of that by the previous owner before we moved in, but thanks just the same."

The neighbor added more surprising news. She asked if the previous owner had told us of the murders that took place in the house.

My mom was shocked by this and answered, "No! I hadn't been informed of that tidbit of information."

This house held two ghosts of the past. One was a very petite woman with short, cropped, mousy-colored hair. She was short in stature, sort of a plain Jane in the looks department. She was first spotted by a detective I had been dating at the time. It was a very cold, crisp winter, deep in snow, and I do mean bone-chilling, to say the least. We were returning from a nice date, which included dinner, a nice chat, and another unmentionable but pleasant event. It was around midnight when we arrived in front of the house. My date did something strange and different from any other time we had been together. He looked at the door of the house and matter-of-factly said, "Well, it looks like your mother is waiting up for you."

Sure I thought after recovering from the initial shock of his words, *but my mother never waits at the door for me—not ever!* With this in mind, I wondered who the hell he was talking about and climbed out of his car. He told me that he had to get on home since he had to get up at four o'clock in the morning. He reminded me to watch my step going through the snow and icy places. I started to pick my way from the curb to the house and, as I was waving goodbye, I turned my gaze toward the door. Lo and behold, for the first time ever, I finally got a look at one of the ghostly apparitions of the people who had been murdered in the house. This ghost looked like she might be somewhere between her late twenties and her early forties. All I know is that she didn't appear to be very old.

What struck me as funny was that she held back the mint green, opaque curtain at the front door. She was standing there and looking at me with very worried, sad eyes—very much like a worried mother. When I finally made it to the porch, I was truly wondering if she might be a houseguest visiting with Mom.

This was just a logical take on the situation. You see, no one wants to think they're being watched by a dead person. But alas, to my horror, this babe was no houseguest. She was one of the unfortunate victims of foul play, about whom the neighbor had spoken earlier.

The apparition disappeared before I got to the door. I knocked on the window of the house to awaken my mother who slept downstairs, near me, right off of the living room. Sleepy from her rude awakening, Mom let me in. As I came through the door, it hit me that I had just had an encounter with a real live ghost. Or was it a person? Or, an apparition? I left the front door open and sank down on the couch, in a small state of shock. My mom was in a small state of shock of her own, and naturally she questioned my sanity when I left the door open. I had never done that before, especially at such a late hour.

My mother asked, "Were you born in a barn? You know better than to leave the door open like that, especially at this hour of the night." I guess, at that moment, I didn't much care about a living person, or anything else, coming through the door. I was speechless and couldn't even talk and tell her what I had seen!

My mother looked at me and asked, "What's wrong with you? Cat got your tongue?"

Not exactly, mommy dearest. She leaned forward to get a closer look at my face, and then she drew back with astonishment. She saw that I was not myself. She then said to me, "My God, you look white as a sheet, like you've seen a ghost!"

I slowly looked up and spoke. "Mom, I did see a ghost." At that, my mother told me to quit babbling like an idiot and go to bed. Retiring to our bed, I finally settled down to sleep when a noise came from the room right above us. Dad and the boys were at work at that time, or they were in their own homes. The noise was that of someone sitting up in bed, putting on what sounded like heavy combat boots, and walking across the bedroom and into the hall. It was headed to the bedroom across the hall. It sounded like it started opening a window, and then it opened another one two seconds later. Then, just as quickly as they were opened, they were closed again.

I softly touched my mother's arm and asked if she heard it, too. She replied that she had. Then we listened for more sounds. We were not waiting long before "Mrs. Ghost" exited that room, turned to the left, and walked a short distance down the hall, past the closet. She passed the bathroom. We were relieved that she turned instead of coming down the stairway, which she had to pass to get to the bathroom.

Phew I thought, *what a relief.* It walked into the bathroom and closed the door. No other sound emanated from the room. Then the walking continued, as she came out of the bathroom and went back to the bedroom she had come from. After going back into the room, she took those lead boots off, and one by one, *thud, thud*, dropped those loud, noisy suckers to the floor.

Mom and I were beside ourselves, completely and utterly perplexed, and we didn't know what to do. Since the snow was deep and the temperature outside was dropping, we were in a creek without a paddle, so to speak. Mom and I sat in the bed, trying to figure out what the heck to do, when all of a sudden, the ghost started on another trek. This time, she got up from the bed and started toward the closet door of our bedroom. She began moving things around on the shelf. She went ballistic on us, knocking things around in a rage. I told Mom that I'd had enough of "Mrs. Spooks" and wanted to get out of Dodge. Mom could come or stay; I just wanted out of there. Mom said that maybe it would be wise to get out of there. Duh!

Then, as fast as she had agreed, she recanted, "No way, José! I'm not freezing my lily pad for nothing, not even a ghost."

After a bit, the ghost left the room and proceeded down the hallway. Mama suggested I go check out the scene and find out what, or who, this ghostly intruder was. *Yeah right, Mama, you betcha. I'll be glad to risk life and limb to check out a lifeless being that, at any time, could appear (or disappear) and clobber me as I keel over from pure fright. Yep, indeedy-do!* I was told to investigate, so I arose slowly and started toward the French doors that led to the living room. I continued past the fireplace and the dining area, until I arrived at the stairs.

I stood at the foot of the stairs and looked upward, watching for the unknown "guest," and then I started up the steps. I got about three steps up, when I heard the eerie footsteps starting to come down the stairs. *Help! This is the craziest thing I could be doing.* So away I went, sprinting down the steps and throwing myself on the bed.

Mom, in the meantime, was wondering what had caused my reaction, and of course, as any fool should be able to guess, it was obvious what had caused my reaction, wasn't it? But thank heavens, the ghost didn't come all the way down the stairs. Instead, she went back to that room. After talking it over, my mom and I decided to get some sleep.

❖

THE FRANKENSTEIN MONSTER

One cold winter night, one of my seven brothers decided to make some delicious fudge. Because we didn't have a refrigerator back in the 1940s, we had to purchase ice blocks for our ice box. It was late at night, and even though Mom had placed the card out on the porch asking the ice man to bring more ice, we wouldn't have any until morning. My brother said that, since there was no ice, he'd use the back stoop of the house to freeze the fudge.

My brother carried the delicious platters of yummy fudge to the back of the house. He opened the back door and put the first plate on the stoop. He turned and reached for the second plate. As he was leaning over with this plate, he quickly straightened up with a start and ran back into the house with a perplexed look on his face. Naturally, the rest of us were curious about what had led him to do such an unusual thing.

After a few seconds, my brother composed himself and explained what had happened. He said, for all to hear, that when he stooped to put the fudge down, he happened to look over at the alley to the left of our house. On the other side of our neighbor's house, my brother saw a vision that could be found only in a nightmare or a horror movie. There, in the alley, moving at a very slow snail's pace, was a tall, square-headed monster, like the one Mary Shelley described in her book, *Frankenstein.* It looked like an ogre, and it was carrying what appeared to be a female in a flowing white gown.

Leaving us with that description, he decided to try to find out what it was and to see if he could rescue the damsel in distress, so to speak.

My other brother decided to join him, and off they went. Of course, I thought I had to go too, but that idea was quickly put to rest, as the boys didn't want a sissy girl who might possibly scare away the monster, whatever it was.

Undeterred, I trailed after them, without their knowledge, to the mouth of the alley. The boys were looking here and there. "It" had apparently disappeared from sight, as if by some sort of magic. Satisfied that nothing was there, the boys and I returned, and we settled down to warm, great-tasting fudge.

The Slamming Doors

It was a very quiet night. In the heat of the summer, nothing was stirring, not even a mouse (oops, wrong season folks, sorry about that). It was deathly still and very eerie this particular evening. My sister-in-law, three of my brothers, my mother, and I were in the house at the time that the next ghostly episode took place.

We were talking, laughing, and enjoying ourselves while we ate snacks and drank coffee or tea. All of a sudden, at the witching hour, or close to it, a door slammed off its hinges and shook the entire eight-room house. We stopped at once and sat in shock. As I said before, there was no activity in the air at all; it was hot and deathly still—not even a window was open. A little murmuring took place, and then we decided to see what was going on up stairs.

Arming ourselves with various weapons, of sorts—a knife, a shoe, whatever we could muster—we crept up the stairs. After arriving at the hall level of the house, we slowly tried each and every door. There was a hall closet in the center of the hall, a bathroom on one side of the closet, and a bedroom on the other. We proceeded down the hall to the bedroom, where we thought the noise was coming from, and the funny thing about it, was that prior to this evening, this door, like all the other doors, would not stick when closed. The door just would not stay tight.

But on this evening, we were shocked to find it shut tight, as if someone had locked it. No matter how hard we pushed, it would not open. Then we pushed on the hall closet and found it to be the same as the other. It would not open, no matter what. It was locked by an apparition, who would display anger at times but seemed protective and fond of me.

It was a mystery that could not be solved by anyone, so we just tried to deal with the stuck doors while we went back to talking, this time about an "unearthly one."

The Dismembered Arm

It was a quiet night in the summer. My mom and I went to bed, and I usually slept on my stomach, as I was more comfortable that way. Typically, I would lay awake, thinking about the events that had taken place, relishing in some and discounting the rest.

Well, on this particular night, as I lay counting sheep, I felt a hand on my rump. It was a very slow, rhythmic beat on my butt, like that of a loving person letting you know how much they care.

I was still for a while and thought that it had to be Mom. But knowing, too, that Mom and I were not that close, I put a halt to that idea. I then wondered who else it could be? Slowly, pulling myself on my elbows, I propped myself up and looked over at Mom. I sleepily decided that there was no way this could be her, unless she had extra arms growing out of her back. She was sleeping with her back toward me and with both arms folded in front of her. Plus, she was asleep.

I then turned slowly and saw the forearm of the small lady. There was no body; there was just an arm wearing a tight, black sleeve with pink floral print, and the third finger was slipped through a loop in the sleeve. It was the sleeve of a dress used to bury women during the time period in which she was murdered. The hand patted me slowly, and then it was gone—*poof*!

A Burglar? I Think Not.

The ghost woman seemed to worry and fret over me as if I were her own. Several members of the family lived in the house, and of course, I was one of them. Downstairs, one of my brothers was wisecracking and making us laugh. All of a sudden, my other brother came from upstairs, where he had been reading, and caught our attention because he was stiff legged in one leg. He looked like Festus from *Gunsmoke*. My brother and I caught sight of this goofball, and we stopped in our tracks. We were surprised at such a sight because nothing had been wrong with his leg before.

My brother asked Goofy about the stiff-leg bit, to which the limping brother replied angrily, "Be quiet! I have a rifle down my pants, so hush up."

My brother downstairs asked him why he stuffed a rifle down his pants leg. Again, he was told to be quiet, and that there was a burglar outside. He saw and heard him. The brother downstairs suggested that the other brother had better think twice about going out and causing the burglar to drop dead of laughter when he raised his leg to shoot the intruder. He might end up blowing off his own foot instead.

The burglar turned out to be the male ghost, who disappeared into thin air.

THE PEEPING SPIRIT

One summer night, after returning from a date with a boyfriend, I knew that I was coming down with the whooping cough or croup. I remember that I was about twenty-one years old, at the time. After being dropped off, I darted up the porch stairs and inside as quickly as I could. Inside, I began coughing in a very deep, hoarse voice. I went to lie in bed with Mom, but I couldn't stop coughing. Unable to go back to sleep, my dear, sweet mother told me to swallow a tablespoon of honey to help stop the barking sounds of my cough.

The moon was full and bright enough that I didn't have to turn on the kitchen light. I took out the honey jar and poured a tablespoon of the sticky stuff onto my spoon. I swallowed the golden nectar and went to shut the cabinet door, when I was overcome by the feeling that someone was watching me. The hairs on the nape of my neck stood up at attention, and I froze in my tracks.

Slowly turning toward the next-door neighbor's house, I looked out of the kitchen window, and there, before my eyes, stood a man (or, so I thought) wearing a suit. He did not move a muscle; he stood stone still. He just stared straight at me without blinking an eye. Of course, I did some moving, and it was quick moving, at that. My mother wanted to know why I made a beeline back into bed. I told her, and she told me to go back to sleep, as usual.

WRESTLING WITH THE MIDDLETOWN CEMETERY GHOST

The summer day was boring, and there wasn't much to do. My brother nearest to me in age and I decided we'd go to his friend's house. I was a tomboy deluxe at an early age and liked to be with my brother and his friends. My brother and I, along with a posse of about five or six boys, decided we'd go up by the Big Four railroad tracks and see what we could get into. We found a spot, by the tracks, directly across from the Middletown Cemetery. This was one of the oldest cemeteries in the city, with grave markers dating back as far as the seventeenth century.

Just before midnight, we were standing by the tracks, laughing and cutting up, when one of the boys looked straight down the tracks. He began talking loud and fast, pointing incessantly, and saying, "Oh, my God! Look at that coming down the tracks! What the hell is it?"

We all stopped to look in the direction he was pointing; what we saw coming down the tracks was a tall, white, misty, and shapely ghost of a woman. She was moving slowly down the tracks. We were directly in her path, and she was closing in on us. We were frozen in utter fear and shock. Then she just vanished into thin air, right before she reached the spot where we were standing.

One of the boys was then wrestled to the ground by the ghost. While our friend was screaming and fighting for dear life, we watched helplessly, as we didn't know what to do. We were going to turn and run when my brother decided to help in some way. He began pelting the ghost with small stones, but because it was a spirit and not solid, the only one phased by the stones was the boy being attacked by the spirit! The boy cried out for my brother to stop. Soon after my brother stopped throwing stones, the boy was released. He quickly got to his feet, and we all ran to our homes as quickly as we could.

THE GOOSE-STEPPING GHOST

The Middletown Cemetery was a favorite haunt (excuse the pun). One clear, starry,] summer night, my husband and I decided to walk through the cemetery with two of our friends. We wanted to read the dates on the tombstones, to see how old they were. While my girlfriend and I went further into the cemetery, we didn't pay much attention to the men and what they may have been doing.

At one point, thought, I looked around, and they were nowhere to be seen. My girlfriend and I were in the center of this historic plot of aged bones and undying spirits by ourselves! We decided to get out of there, and we started down the path toward the open gates. As we proceeded along the path, we approached a mausoleum, which housed the remains of a man who had died of some illness. As we neared the tomb, we caught sight of a man, as solid as any living person, standing there and facing our way. He wasn't looking at anyone or anything in particular; he was just staring, like a statue.

He had on tight pants and a shirt that opened almost to the bellybutton. As we got closer, he turned, stared at the tomb for a second or two, and marched the goose step (like a German soldier) right through the wall of the tomb. We found our husbands hiding and waiting to scare us, but the gentleman inside the graveyard had already done the job for them.

The Cemetery Dare

Once again, the Middletown Cemetery is the backdrop to one of my many hauntings. It was, indeed, one of the most haunted places you could ever visit.

I was, and will always be, a tomboy at heart; I had seven brothers and no sisters. I preferred being around boys who were older than I was. One of my brothers was about two years my senior, and we loved being adventurous. We went looking for ghosts, or anything exciting that we could find.

One evening in particular, we went to the cemetery at about 11:30 pm. We wanted to go in, but we were too scared. After twenty minutes passed, one of the guys with us (usually, there were seven or eight of us who hung out together) dared someone to go into the cemetery alone. The dare required a person to go all the way to the back of the cemetery, walk among the gravesites, and then come out.

Being the tomboy that I was at that age, I could run fast, jump high, and fight the best of them. In other words, I thought I was invincible. Naturally, I volunteered to go into the cemetery all by myself.

I began my dark tour through this final resting place of many souls. I went all the way to the back, and I admit it that I was scared out of my wits! It also didn't help that I passed a really tall monument and mistook it for a monster! I had just passed it by when, all of a sudden, I heard a rumbling and felt a tremor under my feet. I turned to see what was going on, and the monument appeared to be uprooting itself, as if it were a tree. When it fell onto the ground, I almost fainted.

I told my legs to start moving as fast as they could go. I found my way over flat headstones, half stumbling, half running, and made a beeline to the eight-foot fence surrounding the cemetery. I finally cleared the graves and, as I was running toward the boys on the other side of the fence, I had to make a decision: climb the fence, or run all the way around to the entrance. The choice was quite clear. I climbed—or, just about jumped— over the fence!

The experiences that I had had throughout my younger years would make your hair stand on end. But I enjoyed every one of them!

FOLLOW THE SOUND OF THE FOOTSTEPS

And then there was another incident from "The House that Mr. and Mrs. Ghost Built" in Ohio. I was just dating the fellow who was to become my husband. He was home on leave from the Marine Corps, and we had been out on a date that day. Night was now falling all around us, as we walked to my house. We wanted to spend as much time together as possible, because he was shipping out to Vietnam the next day.

We finally arrived at my house and decided to spend this last night together, on the porch. My mother agreed to our plan and soon went to bed. My Marine and I cozied up in a lounge chair to go to sleep. I sat between his legs as he laid back. He wore his dress blues, which I adored on him. He looked so dashing and handsome, but my Marine didn't like the dress blues. He said the stiff collar held his neck in a very straight position. He said it forced his head to be held high and to make him look proud!

We lay back in the lounge chair and were beginning to get comfortable when, out of the blue, came a big loud *thud* in the rose bushes in front of the porch. It was right there next to us! It sounded like an elephant had fallen into the bushes, and it scared the *you know what* out of us. My Marine jumped to his feet, and in doing so, he knocked me up on mine.

It was a great mystery for the two of us. He checked it out, and so did I; we found nothing out of place. It was too much to take in, believe me!

After nothing appeared to be out of place, we decided to try settling down again. When we were positioned cozily in the same place again, we heard another loud *thud*. It was the same sound as before. Then we began hearing tiny, quick footsteps darting down the driveway. It sounded like the short staccato steps of a tiny lady. Whatever was causing the sound was moving down the driveway, toward the front of the house, as if it were coming out of the garage and heading to the front door. As we listened to the footsteps, we both sat up on the lounge, watching to see what we could see.

Whatever it was came to the front and started up the porch steps. We were still thinking that we would see something, but it was not visible to the human eye. We listened to the steps going to the door, and to the door opening and closing, but nothing was ever seen. "It" pinched my boyfriend, twice. At first, he thought I was pinching him, but he realized it wasn't me when he saw that my hands were in front of me and couldn't have reached him. "It" was finally seen walking, from the downstairs bedroom, as a shadowy, dark figure of a small woman. She was heading toward the stairs and through the living room,.

"A Restless Soul"

After twenty-four years of living in Middletown, Ohio, I moved to Florida with my Marine (who had now become my husband). I had one child, and she was with her grandparents, who had previously moved to Florida. As the years passed, I divorced and remarried (he is still with me today), and we moved to Webster, Florida in the year 2000. We bought a very pretty three-bedroom, one-bath home on an acre of land. It had a small porch, and we'd sit out in the nice screened-in room listening to music.

My eyes were about to pop out of my head as he neared the truck, and finally, my husband took notice of my facial expression. He turned and looked at the apparition, and his mouth flew open in disbelief! He was scared out of his wits and made a mad dash for his truck and then left.

There are many more stories and events that took place in my life, and they all were similar to the stories I have put forth to you now. These are the ones that I have chosen to put down on paper for you. I have had one hell of a life; it has been amazing. I hope you enjoyed reading these stories as much as I enjoyed writing them.

Happy reading!

A Man with No Face

In my bed one night, my husband was sleeping soundly beside me as I restlessly tried to fall asleep.

I happened to glance down, toward the foot of my bed, and to my utter surprise, I saw what appeared to be a man standing sideways in front of our master.

He wore pants and a short-sleeved shirt; and he stood about 5'9" tall. When I got a good look at his face, it was horrifying in sight. His face appeared to have big holes in it—jagged, circular-shaped areas on his face.

He was disgusting to look at, to say the least.

I watched in dismay as he, ever so slowly, moved toward the bathroom and disappeared into the darkness of the room.

Another rather eerie incident occurred a short while after that.

This time, I was again lying restlessly in bed, when all of a sudden, out of nowhere, a pair of hands began wrapping themselves around the ankle of my left leg.

The hands were gentle, but I was not accustomed to apparitions touching my body parts. So, I just as gently slipped away from the hands.

It was on a cold winter night when I was, again, in bed and, yes, I had trouble sleeping. (I've had these problems since I was seven years old.) I was turning in for the night, and as usual, my husband was asleep. I was starting to get as comfortable as possible when I felt a cool breeze slowly coming up my side, toward my face.

When it closed in on my face, it became more of a cold breeze, very frigid and icy. It nearly froze my face, as it started suffocating me. Then I became alarmed and slid my face under the blankets.

After a while, the cold air finally died away, but similar occurrences happened later on.

Quite frequently, there have been heavy boots walking slowly on our porch, and it still goes on at times. It sounds as though someone is walking up to the door, but then he or she decides to walk away. It is just a few steps, but when I go to see who's doing the heavy stepping, there is no one to be seen at all.

Things have been known to go missing without cause. Even when objects are under lock and key, they often come up missing, as do clothes and recently-bought food supplies. We might go off somewhere, come back, go to the pantry to get something to eat, and—*bingo*—find that the food is gone.

My hubby and I might be watching TV when, all of a sudden, we hear a loud crashing sound. Or, we might see an object fall when, in fact, there would be no way it could do this. It might be an object which was secured in such a way that nothing could've caused the fall, unless the object was physically pushed.

When we have been away for awhile, on returning we have found our pets' cages on the ground, taken apart, as if someone angrily knocked them over. The animals have been cowering in various places, scared out of their wits. Once, the cage of our pet bird was on the floor and torn apart from a strong shove or push.

Something is haunting us.

I have had ghostly encounters all my life, and they have been very thrilling. My brother, his friends, and I often went ghost hunting, and we found, at times, more than our share of thrills and excitement.

For example, the Big Four Railroad tracks were a great place for ghosts.

For instance, there was the mystery train. One night, my brother Jim, the boys, and I went hunting for our favorite things–ghosts. We were playing by walking directly on the tracks. As I had great balance, I was playing the game quite well. But all of a sudden, one of the boys yelled out, "What the hell?"

Startled by his loud voice, I jumped off the track, and then he yelled, to everyone, "Get off the tracks!"

Everyone looked straight ahead where there appeared to be a train coming our way. There was the mournful sound of the whistle, the churning sound of the engine, and the bright shine of the headlights.

We jumped off the tracks to yield to the oncoming train. Some jumped on one side of the track, and the rest of us jumped on the other.

As the train approached, we looked to see a train glide between the two groups. But instead of seeing a train, we were looking at each other.

To our amazement we just stared at one ghostly train, with sounds and lights. How's that for excitement, folks?

Again, when we went searching for spooks, we often went to the Middletown Cemetery. We trudged through, looking at old, and I mean *old*, tombstones.

It was interesting, and we liked adventures, anyway. As we were walking along, I happened to look skyward, and I saw three ghosts flying over the cemetery. Like Casper, the Friendly Ghost, they were white and misty. Unlike Casper, they were not smiling. I told the boys, and we left in a hurry.

My husband, Buddy, and I were renting a house in Montverde, Florida, which was originally was owned by an elderly couple.

One night, when we were in bed, he was asleep, while I lay there, awake. In the back yard, a strange something could be seen through our bedroom window. Next, I heard the cry of a wolf howling, such as what you might see or hear in a movie about a werewolf.

I slowly got the courage to roll over and wake up my husband. We listened together, and he also heard the sound of a baying wolf.

We couldn't explain what happened. It occurred very late at night—on a night to remember, that is.

In that same house, while in bed at night, we saw a small light come from the doorway of the bedroom. It glided along the wall, creeping along until it was on the other side of the bed, which my husband slept on. Then it grew into a bigger light and?

Afterward, it slowly shrank in size, and then it left the room the same way it came in.

The light appeared at different times, and sometimes there were two lights. They changed from small to larger sizes after entering our room.

They came in the door of the bedroom and moved slowly along the wall. Then they went back out again.

I figured it was the old couple coming back from beyond the grave to see who was now in their home. Then one night, we were in bed, and I was on the side of the bed nearest to a built-in chest of drawers. Only two drawers opened easily enough to use. The very bottom one—there were three all together—would not open at all. For some reason or other, the fool ???????

As I was saying, this drawer was as stubborn as a mule and would not budge. On this one night, we retired kind of early, and in a little while, my husband conked out and went to sleep. As usual, I lay awake, counting stars in the sky, when all of a sudden, all hell broke loose. The third drawer, that wouldn't budge at all, budged all night. It flew from out of the wall with the loudest bang and clutter. I jumped out of my skin, and when I turned to wake up my husband, he told me that he already heard it. We got up, and I turned on the light and looked where the noise had ???????????

We found that the drawer was out on the floor, and there was no way we could figure out how this could've happened. When I was told about the two old people being the previous owners, I felt it had been them, coming back to their home. We were told they loved this home. So I guess they didn't want us living there and they were trying to scare us enough to make us move.

I had been at my cousin Anneta's house for the summer. She lived with her father, mother, brother, and sister on a farm in Indiana. I lived in Ohio. I was in my early teens, and so was she. We got along beautifully for a while, until I got homesick. My cousin Sammy, Annetta's brother, and I had a ball, too. We played in the rain and my ?????????? cow. I was a city slicker, so I didn't know how this was done. But to everyone's amazement, including my own, I did the job like a pro. He laughed and said, "That was really something because it took a special way to do it."

But I did it, nonetheless.

The two-story farmhouse had a bed for everyone but me to sleep in. I was asked to sleep on the couch. I didn't feel comfortable in strange places and was very frightened at the thought of sleeping there alone. But I didn't want to cause any trouble, so I went to lie down on the couch downstairs, all by my lonesome, while everyone else was upstairs.

I lay in a puddle of fear and sweat as I tried to tell myself, *hey, this is my uncle Orville and aunt Fanny's house. Why should I be scared of their old farmhouse?*

The hair on the back of my neck started standing up at attention. I lay as still as I could, so as not to draw the attention of whatever may be lurking there. All of a sudden, I heard footsteps quietly walking in the living room. I couldn't move; fear wouldn't let me.

Finally, the next day, I told Annetta about my fear of sleeping alone, and she said I could sleep with her in her bedroom. Was I ever relieved! We did each other up, with makeup and hairstyling, in Annetta's room, and I enjoyed those moments so very much.

On the first night I slept in with Annetta, she and I said, "Goodnight," and we turned out the light. Oh boy, was it dark! I lay in the inky-dark room, and this chillingly fearful feeling come over me.

While my cousin lay sleeping peacefully, I was awake, as usual. I closed my eyes, attempting to get a little shut-eye, I heard a movement in the room. I didn't know what to make of it or what to do: whether to wake Annetta or leave her be. I just lay quietly hoping that this would soon go away, but to my dismay, it only got worse. I began to hear and feel scratching on the top part of the bed. It was like a hand scratching on the bed, just above my pillow. As I started a slow panic-attack, the thing came closer to my head, and then I heard a breathing sound right in my right ear. Was I afraid or what? You betcha! I was scared out of my wits, I tell you.

I didn't dare move. This thing breathed right on my face, and then I felt light touches after the breathing. I was fit to be tied and was glad it finally stopped.

I told Annette the next day. She only laughed and said I must have been asleep. *Yeah! In your dreams, sweet cousin.* I left for home soon after, and I was glad to get away from there, believe me!

I had an experience, when I was in my teens and still living in my hometown of Middletown, Ohio.

I was walking one pretty, sunny afternoon to visit a friend. On my walk I noticed that no one but me was out on the street. Now and then, a straggler might happen by, but they were few and far between. As I strolled along, I happened to see this young man walking slowly toward me. I didn't pay too much attention at first. He approached me, and I noticed that his feet didn't make a sound. Then I began to notice him more closely and found more weird stuff going on.

He didn't blink an eye or walk like a human being. And he never even said anything when I said, "Hi." He walked by like a zombie. I turned to see the back of him, and then *poof* he was gone into thin air. I was amazed to no end and couldn't get over it for a long while.

And then, one hot summer night, my family and I sat around laughing—cutting up and generally just goofing off, you might say. My mother had a chair she claimed as her own, and no one but her sat in it. Get it meathead? (Archie Bunker.) We sat there, chatting, as the time neared 11:00 p.m., when, all of a sudden, coming from outside, came the most eerie voice I've ever heard. All it did was call out one of my brothers name several times. Slowly and mournfully, it called out, "Freddie, Freddie."

We all shut-up and looked at each other, but it quit and was never heard again.

When we were children, my brother Tim, who is two years older than I am, and I were being watched by an older brother.

Brother Jim and I were playing on the floor. My older brother was sitting on the end of the couch. From where he was sitting, he could see straight into the dining room. As we quietly played, my older brother asked, in a quiet but disturbing way, for us to come over to where he was sitting and look at the table.

On the table sat our salt and pepper shakers, which he told us to watch very closely. As we did, we noticed that the pepper shaker was slowly sliding around a small area of the table. Then the salt shaker slowly rose into the air, went upside down, and fell to the table. The pepper shaker did the same. They put on a show like that for a while and then stopped.

As time has passed, I have moved to many states, and in some of the other homes, I have found unexpected guests, if you know what I mean.

At times, I have visited my mother's home. On one particular night, I was in the front room, on a sofa bed, when I saw a movement out of the corner of my eye. So as I lay on my back, I turned my head slowly, and there, coming at me, was a beautiful blonde, dressed in dark slacks and a beautiful, white, long-sleeved blouse. She had long, golden hair that fell down her shoulders in beautiful ringlets. Who she was, or what she was, I don't know. All I know is that she came straight toward the middle of my bed, and walked right through it.

Another tale, of ghostly proportions, took place at a nightclub in Orlando, Florida. My husband and I used to frequent the club because of the great bands and music, as I love to dance. We'd go in and wait eagerly for the band to start, and on one particular night, we were talking to each other when, all of a sudden, the lights near to us went out. Soon after, the waitress came to turn them back on. Every so often, these lights went off and on again. At other times, the candles went go out and have to be relit, over and over.

One night, we were there, and the band started coming in, and we chatted with some of them. On this night, the boys were running around, setting up for their gig, when all of a sudden, the lights went out. The waitress came to turn them on, and everything seemed to be going pretty well, until one of the guys took a chair up on stage to ready the lights. He got off the chair and walked over to another guy, who had called him for some reason. Then that same guy who had been using the chair came back, and when he looked at the chair, he stopped dead in his tracks. I called my husband's attention to it because we weren't certain what was going on with the guy. Then the fellow yelled out, asking who'd poured water on the seat he was using to adjust the lights. As the other guys looked at him, perplexed, and asked what was he talking about. Then he proceeded to tell them that the chair had been dry while he had been standing on it. He even looked up at the ceiling to see if he could see water anywhere. But there wasn't a single drop.

So where does that leave us? Did someone from beyond the grave decide to pee on the seat as a joke? Who knows? Anyway, the poor man was beside himself, and all the guys were left scratching their heads in great wonderment.

On our next visit to the club, the waitress told us of the man who had previously owned the place and how he dearly loved operating the club. He loved to interact with the patrons, and he loved talking and cutting up, as well. She informed me that, after he died, he had been seen on many occasions going about the place as he had done in life. This man had owned a theater, as well, that sat just up the street. He haunted it, too.

The actors and actresses were preparing to go on stage, and they heard footsteps. But when they turned to look, they found nothing there. They saw him in various places, doing whatever he did in life. He was seen in the balcony, sitting and watching the plays in action. Quite a lively guy, wouldn't you say?

At one point, my husband and I were between cars and had to get a cab or walk back and forth to the club. I favored the cab, thank you. Well, anyway, on this one particular night, we were eagerly waiting to dance the night away, when one of the waitresses told me a story. She prefaced by saying that, after closing time, the workers cleaned off the tables, stacked the chairs, and blew all the candles out. They would then disappear into the kitchen, and go about their nightly chores. One night, one of the workers happened to see something very strange as he exited the kitchen.

As he gazed into the lounge area, he noticed flickering lights of eerie proportions. Yes! The candles were relit. Suffice it to say, the poor guy had to stop whatever he was doing and blow the foolish candles out again—and several more times that night, as a matter of fact.

And on a separate occasion, we were having a great time, as usual. We spoke to the owner and to others in the joint, and we danced our legs off. Afterward, we had to call for a cab. So Buddy and I slipped out of the lounge to the pay phone. Buddy crossed the room, in order fetch a cab, and I sat right close to the exit door. To the right of where I sat, down a short hallway, were the men's and women's restrooms. Yes, every night, after closing time, the waitress would come and check the restrooms to see if some drunk had fallen, head-first, into the potty or crashed to the floor, in a stupor.

On this night. she stepped into each restroom, turned out the lights, closed the doors, and walked past me with a smile on her way back into the lounge. Buddy, in the meantime, was still talking to the cab company owner. As I was watching to see if he was about ready to pull the phone from his ear, a slam of a bathroom door jarred me out of my seat. I was stunned for a moment, and when I turned to see what was going on, as usual, there was nothing or no one there, but Mr. Ghost. We finally got a cab and left spooky club for the time being.

We now live in Alabama. As I mentioned before, there are plenty of spooks here, too. My husband and I often sit up at night, for as long as we can stand it, to watch *Ghost Hunters* and *Ghost Adventures*. One night, we were drinking hot chocolate, watching ghost stories experienced by celebrities, and enjoying it very much, when all of a sudden, I felt this icy-cold breeze up my feet and legs. At first, I tried to dismiss it and kept watching the program. But the icy air came further up, and I knew there was no way this could be happening, for we had the heat on, and it was warm. I was beginning to get spooked, and I asked my husband, who sat next to me in his chair, if he could feel it too. He said, "Yes," and then we felt it move up to our faces.

We went to bed to escape the freezing air from the spook I had seen previously.

In Clermont, Florida, my husband and I were going to go for a bike ride. We were idly standing and yakking about where to ride to, when, from up above the roof of the house came this eerie, slow, low speaking voice. It called out both our names, "Shirley, Buddy," and that was it—nothing more. We looked at each other, and then we looked around to see if something was standing nearby. When we realized it had come from the rooftop, we took off on our bikes a little faster than intended, believe me!

In our home, in Alabama, I decided to do some laundry early one evening. Buddy, went into the master bedroom and lay down for a rest. I went to start a load, but I also had to retrieve the soap for the clothes. I returned to the laundry room, which overlooks the backyard. It was getting darker, so I asked my husband to get out of bed to turn the outside lights on. He did just that and returned to the bedroom. I went back to doing my laundry.

As I was loading in the clothes, I had the strong urge to look out the laundry-room door. I looked out the door to the yard and saw nothing, at first. Thinking no more about it, I set to work again. On the third load, I got another strange urge to look out the door. I stepped back to the door, and appearing out of pitch black, came an eerie sight from our neighbor's electrified fence (to keep his cows and horses from leaving their pasture).

I thought, *what in the world?* It came from total darkness and was approaching the light from the shed. It moved very slowly, very much like a zombie, so to speak. It turned out to be a ghostly apparition of a medium-build, snow-white sheep dog. He kept coming very slowly, never batting an eye. He never turned to look to see if anyone or anything was out there.

As he came up, almost to the door where I stood,watching, he lowered his head ever so slowly. I yelled for my husband to check it out, and when I walked back to the door, *poof,* he was gone. My husband went out and searched the whole yard over, but no doggie. I often wonder if it might have been trying to show me where something was, or maybe he himself might be resting there, beneath the sod. Who knows? Right? So much for the pooch; doggone it anyway.

On another occasion, in Middletown, Ohio, I was hanging around with my brothers and six of their friends, and we were playing in the back of our house. I was a tomboy deluxe. I would, and could, outdo most of the guys in knife throwing and all kinds of tricks. I also was the only sister with seven brothers. Now, you can understand why I'd be a tomboy. Anyway, we were wondering how to break the boredom of suburban life. As we were mulling over ideas, I came up with a new game; I had seen a long, thin club-like board and came up with the idea of throwing it, like a spear, at the apricot tree. We also had a cherry tree, but we decided to throw it toward the apricot tree instead. So we began to talk about who would go first, and I let the boys go first, of course. After they threw and missed, I picked up the club, threw it, and *bingo*! I hit it square on. It was fun to see how the boys reacted after their earlier bragging of how "a dumb old girl couldn't hit the side of a barn." They called it beginner's luck, naturally.

After several throws from the boys, I got the last shot. Each and every time I threw, I hit the tree. They missed every time.

But the final time, I took up the club, aimed carefully, and threw. It went as straight as an arrow toward the tree, but this time, the club glanced off the tree, and landed about a foot away from it. It was as though there was a force field around the tree to keep it from being hit.

Stunned and not sure what had just happened, the boys and I tried shaking our fears off as I walked cautiously back toward the tree to try again. This time it was to see if the same thing would happen again. I took the club back to where I'd just came from, took aim, and threw the club at the tree. As usual, it went straight toward the tree, but then it glanced off the tree, again, from about a foot away.

Convinced we were not seeing things, we stood in utter shock to think something as strange as this could really be happening. As we stood in wonder and awe, something suddenly started coming from behind the tree very slowly. At first, it was just a foot and part of a leg. Then out stepped a tall, hairless, and faceless dude, who only had dark spots where his eyes and nose should have been. We were riveted to where we stood, frozen solid with fear. This monster looked down at the club. Then it slowly looked at us. It looked down at the club again and slowly started to pick it up, and as it was doing so, it looked up at us. By the time it had the club in its hands, we felt it was time to do a little picking up, ourselves—of our feet, that is. We couldn't get away fast enough.

On another occasion, in the dead of winter, my brother Richy—who worked the night shift and usually came home quietly so as not to awaken my mother or me—decided, on this night to some in and speak as calmly as possible to awaken my mother.

He asked her if she was awake and she simply replied, "I am now. What do you want?" He said that, as he approached the back door, he saw what appeared to be a man standing in the darkness. My mother said she didn't want to get up because she was comfortable.

He then said he would check it out, but nothing was out there. There was deep snow, yet he could find no shoe tracks. I think it was the male ghost. He seemed to like being outdoors, looking into a window in the backyard area, or just standing like a statue. He just disappeared, as usual.

On another occasion, that same cold winter, my mother and I were in bed when my brother Richy came home from work. I was awake; I heard him turning the key in the back door. My mother was sound asleep, as usual. Richy approached the door to the bedroom, opened it slowly, and this time, his voice was more excitable. He awakened my mother and began to tell of a set of footprints from nowhere, leading to our bedroom window, which overlooked the backyard.

Now, as I said before, the snow was very deep. My mother and I sat up in bed, and she looked at him with concern on her face. Then he told her that the moon was very bright and was shinning down on the white of the snow very much like a spotlight. And that was when he was able to see the footprints clearly. Mom, of course, said next to any ?? of said footprints as it was freezing outside. She told him that she'd see them in the morning, or later. He was visibly shaken by this strange sight, but he finally agreed to wait until the next day.

We went to sleep with a feeling of dread, believe me! Upon rising the next day, my brother eagerly prepared to show Mom and me the footsteps outside our bedroom window. We put on our heavy coats and walked out in shin-deep snow. It was cold, I tell you, and very miserable to be out in that weather. But my brother wouldn't let up, so out we ventured.

We walked around to the window, took a look at these footprints, and nearly fell over in shock. It was like we were in a movie. The footprints sank down deep into the snow, like whatever had made them was itself made of lead. The footprints were as deep as the snow, and then some—they also penetrated through the wet earth beneath the snow. How's that for weight? This dude had to be the same monster my brother and I met with when we were throwing the club at the tree in the backyard. Talk about an electrifying moment—this was it, people.

In amazement, we stood, looking at these giant footprints set. ever so deeply, in the ground. We couldn't begin to fathom the mystery that lay before us on that cold, bone-chilling, winter day.

There was some more spine-tingling news concerning this "big boy" when some teenage kids were strolling along a street that led into town. Late on a summer night, the kids were crossing a street, having an enjoyable time. They got to the other side, and were starting to mosey on down the line, when our friendly neighborhood giant stepped out from behind a big tree. (Of course, we can assume that they turned stone cold from fear, and possibly peed themselves as well. Oh, boy, did they shake in their boots.)

SGathering what little composure they could muster, they found an emergency call box. Shaking to the core, they called for help, and soon a big red fire engine appeared, ready for action. The fire truck arrived to find four hysterical kids talking frantically and all at once. After they told the angry firemen their tale, the firemen told them they couldn't be running around on wild-goose chases and wasting time and money. The kids insisted that their story was true, and they had needed to report it using the call box.

They kindly asked the firemen to dispatch the police to the scene. Slowly, the firemen gave in and did so. When the police arrived and saw kids there, they figured it was a teenage prank that had taken place. In the meantime, the giant vanished, as it always had in the past. The cops soon began to notice real fear in the eyes of these kids. They saw how pale, shaken, and pitiful they looked. Then and there, they took them seriously enough to take down the report, and the incident was reported in the news. This monster got around seemingly ?? in that area for some odd reason.

Another episode of a different sort happened out in the country, when some young teens were taking a romantic ride on a nice summer's day. As they were going along the county road, the radio was on and playing their favorite tunes. All of a sudden, the radio went dead. And, soon after that, the motor died, and the car came to a slow halt. Not knowing what could be wrong, the driver tried fiddling with the radio, and then with the motor to start it, but absolutely nothing happened. A short time later, they found the air full of a very foul odor and wondered *where in the world could this horrid and wretched smell be coming from?* They started looking to see where this stench could be coming from, when a huge creature jumped off of a high hill, landing near the car.

The teens were in total shock, to say the least. This hairy creature had an almost human face and stood about 8' tall,. The windows of the car were closed, and inside, the boy and girl in the front seat were staring at this creature, at close range. It was on the passenger side of the car and

?? to reach through the window where the girl was sitting. The girl wore a sweater over her blouse, and when the creature found that there was a barrier in his way, he got angry and hit the window, breaking through it like sheet of paper. The creature then reached in, grabbed the girl's sweater, and pulled off the sleeve.

Her boyfriend, sitting in the driver's seat, began to go crazy with fear. He jumped out of the car and tried to get the beast away from his sweetie. The he ventured to the back of the car, opened the trunk, and pulled out a baseball bat. He returned to the driver's side of the car, slowly making his way to the front; at which point, he began screaming and brandishing the bat at the hairy beast.

The hairy, man-looking creature was lured away from the passenger side and began to show more interest in the boy. The car kept them apart, and after a short time of David-and-Goliath havoc, the party was over, and the beast lost interest. He turned, and in one giant leap, he was airborne and on top of the high hill.

The shaken lad checked on his friends, and they were okay but very shaken. After a short while, the radio and the engine came back on, and the headlights shone brightly again. Everyone was safe and secure once again. They went on their way with something very interesting to tell about back in town.

In my Ohio home, I was reading the paper in my mother's chair early one evening. The chair was close to the front door, on the right side of the house. On the left side was the entry way to the dining room and kitchen. We had to go between two doors to enter the dining room. The door to the right was a storage closet, and the one on the left led to the full-sized basement. While I sat reading, a huge, loud crashing sound—like that of a wall caving in—came from the basement.

I was alone and frightened out of my ever-loving mind. I jumped out of my skin. I didn't know what to do, or where to go. It was dark outside, and I didn't want to venture far away. Then it came to me—*why don't I go next door to our neighbor, who is usually home in the evening?* So going as fast as my legs could go, I was out of there and on my way to safety. I went to the door and rang the doorbell. Soon, I saw the figure of the man who owned the house coming to the door. He turned the light on, saw it was me, and let me in. I told him I was afraid of being alone in my house and asked if I could stay until my mother or one of my brothers returned.

After I was there for a while, I told him the real reason I had come over. But I told him I didn't want him thinking I was just imagining it, and he said he believed me. He asked if I wanted him to check my house out, and I said he could. We went to my house and, after seeing everything was in order, returned back to his place.

He had been at home alone as well, as his wife and children were away. After a while, I heard a car drive into my driveway and saw the headlights of our car. I thanked him for his kindness and left.

In this same home, on a different day, some of my family members and I were sitting around one evening when my one brother said he heard something out in the backyard. So he decided to go check it out for himself and told us to stay inside. Of course, I waited until he went out the front door to sneak around and slip out. I waited on the porch to see if I could be of any help, as it concerned me very much that he was alone with whatever had made that noise. I was leaning over and could see down to the end of the house and driveway, but my brother was hidden behind the back of the house. It was but a short time before he dashed around the corner and flew to the porch like he had wings on his feet. Out of breath and white as snow, he collected his composure and nervously said he had walked to the back of the house and had run smack-dab into a man.

After several years, he confided in me that the man looked identical to my first husband. He said that the man had run away from him, as well. The other person, or whatever, ran through our backyard, into the neighbor's yard, and down the alley. We lived between two alleys at that time. My first husband and I were split apart by his mean father, who kept him from me. My first husband was intimidated by him and didn't want any trouble for me. But a male ghost was seen by several of my brothers at one time or another, and at nightfall, it is hard to say who is who.

Another strange occurrence happened in Florida, at a mobile home, in which my husband used to live, before we were married. It happened on a quiet summer day, when my husband, then my boyfriend, went out to change the little propane tank that led to his stove. As he was doing so, he glanced over and saw a pant leg, which looked like Elvis Presley's, peek out from behind the mobile home. It was as if Elvis were coming to my boyfriend, but when he turned around fully to encounter Elvis, he had disappeared into thin air.

At that time, I was singing and moving pretty much like Elvis, and I became very popular for it. When I was writing, all of a sudden my pen started moving on its own. It would tell me it was Elvis writing, and he told me a lot of things. I've seen Elvis, after his death, in an apartment in Orlando, Florida. He spoke to me psychically. At various clubs in Florida, people would see Elvis appear in me and say I was him, returned.

My upstairs apartment in Florida was another place of ghostly encounters. It was in an apartment building in downtown Orlando. It consisted of a kitchen, a living room, a bedroom, and a bathroom. I had, at the time, heard the voices of a number of people in the living room when coming up the stairs and unlocking the door. Laughter and voices came from within, and it sounded as though a party was going on.

Another time, my friend Rich and I were in the apartment, having a quiet conversation in the evening. As we sat there, for no reason at all, Rich started crying. I heard soft sobs, so I turned to look in his direction. I found him holding his face in his hands. Knowing that there hadn't been any words between us to cause such an emotion, I didn't know what to say. I was shocked, to say the least.

I gently asked, "Why are you crying, Rich? What is wrong?"

He said, still crying, that his grandfather had died. I thought *why hasn't he said something about it before now?* My attention was turned to the window overlooking the driveway, and while I looked, I saw a dark mist float through the window into the middle of the room. It brought a sad, heavy feeling with it. I began to understand why Rich felt this sadness, because I felt it too. I sat staring at it, wondering what it was. Then a vision came to me in the form of a plague. The plague was characterized by death. After I mentally questioned it further, it replied, somehow, *father*. I took it for granted to mean Rich's grandfather, so I asked if that's what it meant. It said, *no your father.*

I started bawling, without knowing what was going on. The mist left. We both sat in disbelief of what just happened. The next day, I got up, got dressed, and started off to visit my mother and father. I took the bus. When I got off, I crossed the street in the direction of my mother and father's home. I had to walk down a block, and then turn left at the very first street.

As I was walking toward my parents' street, I had this weird premonition that said *your father is dead.* I felt this and knew what to expect upon arriving at their home. I was feeling very sad and scared that this might be true. As I rounded the corner, I saw family members' cars in the driveway, and it was becoming a reality. I entered the house with a sad and heavy feeling of doom. I heard my family's voices, talking until I came into the fold, and everything went deathly still. My mother was on the couch in the living room, and my two brothers were in separate places. One brother was in my mother's chair, in the family room, by himself, although he could still see into the living room. The other brother was sitting on the other couch in the living room.

I walked to the space between them, and then the brother sitting in the family room said, "I guess I will be the one to tell her. Shirley, Dad is gone."

I already knew it—the dark-mist messenger of death had communicated as much the night before. Nonetheless, it was a blow in the gut to me and sent me running into my mother's bedroom, slinging myself across the bed in great sobs. My one brother, who had been sitting in the same room as Mom, came in to comfort me.

After that, my father appeared to me when I was alone and living in the apartment in Orlando. I was preparing to go to bed, the first time I noticed him. I had just crawled into bed, when all of a sudden, I felt my head collide with a hard surface. I thought, logically, *it could be the wall, but then again, how could that be when I was just crawling into the bed? My head would only be midway into the bed.*

I slowly looked up, and to my great amazement, standing there in the center of the bed, like a statue, was my father. He just stood motionless, staring into the room, and then *poof!* He was gone in the blink of an eye.

Another event took place in the same apartment after my father's death, of course. I was going out with a very polite and sweet guy at the time. He came up and kept me company sometimes, and we'd have something to eat and drink. One early evening, he came by with one of his friends. He introduced him to me, and I asked if I could fix something for them. My boyfriend told me to just sit and rest, and that I'd already done enough; now it would be his turn to wash the few dishes after we'd eaten, and I did just that. We gathered in the kitchen, while my boyfriend washed the dishes. His friend and I sat in front of the one window in the kitchen. His friend faced the window head-on, and I faced it sideways.

As we quietly talked, my boyfriend's friend began looking out the window, with a strange look on his face. I noticed it, and then he said, in a matter of-fact voice, "Well, it has to be a giant, or this guy can fly."

Before I could ask what he was talking about, my boyfriend, who was very thoughtful and protective of me, told his friend to button his lip, so as not to frighten me. But I had to know what it was like, and so I asked this friend to describe the thing to me. The window overlooked the fire escape, and it was two stories up to the door and window. So this dude had to have wings or was a giant. Then he told me that he had white hair, gray, two-piece work clothes with short sleeves—what a man might wear to work around the house.

I knew, right off the bat, this was my father and told them so. No one spoke for a spell.

After my divorce, when my daughter and I were staying at my mother's home in Orlando, we were waiting for *The Carol Burnett Show* to come on, as we loved to watch it together. Well, my mother had a dog at the time named Benji, who trailed after Mom at bedtime, without fail. Not on this particular night, though, because on this night, Benji had other ideas. No matter how hard Mom tried to get him to come from the family room, he would not budge. We couldn't figure out why the little guy wouldn't come out, so Mom just gave up on him and went to bed alone.

In the meantime, my daughter and I settled back on one of the two sofas in the living room. As the program came on, the dog began growling and barking in the family room. Not knowing what was going on, we tried to watch the show, but the dog's barking and growling was very loud. Then all of a sudden, all hell broke loose—he came flying out faster than we'd ever seen him go and flew across the floor, like he was on roller skates. He flew to the big picture window in the living room, and pushed his head under the curtain, raging at whatever it was out there. The hair on his neck stood up, to boot.

I felt fear coming over me, and I was beginning to think it could be a supernatural being of some sort. In addition to my father, one of my brothers had died. I asked my daughter if she'd take a peek to see what it could be, and she told me to shove that idea. So I slowly got up, went to where the dog was, and watched which direction he was staring in. I gently and slowly pulled back the drape, just enough to see what was causing all the noise, and followed the dog's gaze. When I did, I saw Benji was staring toward Mom's mailbox and what stood behind it. It was a dark figure, standing there and staring at our window. It was like a statue and had the shape of a man. It brought to my mind a picture of my dead brother. I again started to move toward the couch only this time ????????????

My brother liked visiting with his mother a lot, and I had the very strong feeling that he, the ghostly man outside, was here visiting his mother's house.

Here, in Alabama, my husband and I have had weird goings-on in our house, such as the man with the blackened circles in his ugly mug, cold—and I do mean extremely cold—air slowly rising upon me, the cages of our three pets knocked over, and the animals out and hiding. My husband and I might come from somewhere and, low and behold, there are three wrecked cages, like someone or something knocked the little guys down in a rage and sent them reeling into the air and, *plop*, to the ground. Naturally, the first one I suspect would be the blackened faced boy I've seen standing in front of the John, and in front of the cages. He was turned sideways from me, but the mug was turned to look at the animals. Things have gone missing, only to be found later in the same place, and noises have been heard, like big booms, which are like bombs exploding. These noises could only be made by a ghost.

Wherever I go, there have been things of strange origin. I have seen ghostly shapes in my bedroom lots of times. When I open my eyes at night and look up at the ceiling, a ghost of a man is moving by my bed, and then he is gone into thin air. The thing that I can't understand is why I am always encounter these beings from beyond.

The graveyards have been a source of surprise meetings with ghosts. One such occasion was in Winter Park, Florida, at the Glenn Haven Cemetery. My husband, Buddy, and I went there as often as we could to visit the wall that contains the ashes of my mother, my brother Jim, my father, and my grandchild. One day, we went there, and I went to the wall, while my husband went looking at tombstones. I watched as he traveled quite far. I stood and then sat on a cement bench provided for people to share time with loved ones. As I started to contemplate my huge losses, I looked to see where Buddy was, as he was still walking amongst the gravestones. I wanted to let him know I was ready to leave, when I spotted a woman who had come out of nowhere to be near my husband.

I didn't think too much about it at the time, but it didn't take long to realize that she had surprisingly appeared suddenly and suspiciously. I then watched to see that they didn't look or speak to each other. I knew something was wrong, because my hubby loves to talk and finds no one to be a stranger. The woman,was starting to move between tombstones toward the road. When she arrived at the road, she walked toward the office in the back of the cemetery and vanished.

I told my husband about her, and he said he hadn't seen her at all.

This ghostly encounter took place in Alabama, where we now still reside. One warm day, Buddy and I decided to take advantage of this beautiful summer day and take a walk around the area. We started out talking and discussing different subjects, and we soon arrived at the end of our road. Then we proceeded to the left and on down, until we reached the lane with the brick homes. We slowly made our way along, noticing no one was at home, and we just chatted some more. We only saw one man in front of his house. There was a "For Sale" sign in front of this house, as well. We smiled, waved, and kept going.

We began to tire and started back to go home. For fear of slipping and falling, I would, at times, look down and watch for loose stones or small holes in the road. We were passing the home where we had seen the only man in the neighborhood. Again, I checked for loose stones, and I had already seen that no one was on the outside. But as I looked up from the road, I saw a young woman standing on the porch, leaning against a column of the house.

She looked very sad and forlorn, almost lost. I felt sorry for her and was going to say, "Hi," and maybe perk her up, but after I looked down once more, we came parallel with the house, and no one was there. She disappeared in an instant, and I began to think maybe she had died of suicide or bad health; for the way she looked, it seemed very possible one or the other had taken place. The main thing I noticed was that she didn't move a finger or bat an eyelid. She was, indeed, a spook.

This next event took place in Clermont, Florida. My husband and I were renting a mobile home at the time, and we had been there about a year. We had several pets and loved to go dancing at a local nightspot close by.

We were getting up early, as usual, as my husband had to go to work. On this one morning, he left, and I thought I'd go for a morning stroll. I slowly stepped out and turned to lock the door, but in doing so, I saw a white substance on the doorknob. I didn't think my husband left it there, as he wouldn't be sticking his hands in a white paste. I was not sure what the deal was, and then a pang of fear hit me. Was it poison or something to scare the pants off of me? I collected myself and called the sheriff's station for help. The sheriff looked and told me to stay outside and call my husband. A little later, a big white van pulled up. A husky dude pulled up to the sheriff sitting in his car and quietly spoke for a short while. Then the sheriff left. The big guy rolled on a little further and stopped.

He asked me what was going on, and I showed him the pasty white stuff on the knob. He asked where my husband was, and I told him, "At work."

He returned to his van and proceeded to change into a white outfit worn as protection from hazardous material. He looked like someone in a space outfit. He took a sample, put it into a small vile, and placed it into the back of the van. He then instructed me to get some rags, soap, and warm water, and then clean it off. After the knob was clean, he told me to wash and dry my hands really well. Soon after, he changed his clothes and left.

A few days later, an FBI agent came to my door and asked if I knew of anyone who would want to harm me. I said, "Not that I know of." He said they were sending the white substance to various places, to see what it could be. I then asked, "Do you have any idea what it could be?"

He simply said, "Not yet."

A few days later the same FBI agent came back, this time with a partner. When I opened the door, he just stood there looking very puzzled. So I asked if anything new had been discovered, and he just said, "No."

Then he asked me if I knew what the powder could've been, and I said I didn't. At that point, I asked, "Did anyone find anything out yet?"

He said that they had sent it everywhere possible to check it out and the only thing they knew was that this substance was like nothing they'd ever seen.

I asked, "Do you think it was of this earth?"

He then told me it was not of this earth, and they did not know what it was or where it came from. How's that for a very eerie tale?

This event took place here where my 'old' man and I now dwell, in good old Alabama.

We live in a county called Limestone, and it is beautiful, to say the least. We've resided here for about six years and love living in the country.

The double-wide in which we live is quite large, but as I've mentioned before, it is rather haunted. One evening, my husband and I decided to retire kind of early. Sometimes we listen to music to relax to, or police ?????????

After turning out the light, we talked for a short time and then decided to get some shut-eye.

I turned over on my right side, and then I faced a closet. It was a big closet that required assembly. As I was starting to fall asleep, I happened to turn a little bit more, to get more comfortable, and then I opened my eyes to ask my husband a question. Out of nowhere came a well-built, handsome man who was right there, almost on top of me. He was coming at me and did not seem to know I was there. (He didn't give a hoot either, it seems.) He was looking straight ahead as he walked right past me.

The interesting part about it was that he was as naked as a jaybird—not nary a stitch of clothes on him but close enough to touch. I wouldn't dare, of course. He could only be seen. He was quite dark and muscular. But he was void of any existence, I think. Then *poof!*, he was gone.

Epilogue [or, if this category changes to memoir or autobiography, it should probably be called a Postscript]

The encounters I have had in my life may be unbelievable to most, and frankly, they have been to me, too.

This could have been the thickest book in the world if I had related all of my experiences, but I'm afraid my poor hands could not stand so much writing.

These events are just a small portion of all that I've seen and heard, and I hope you enjoyed reading the stories I have compiled together for your entertainment. Being sensitive to these ghostly encounters has added something to my life, making it special and less boring, to say the least.

Before you turn off your lights for the night, make sure you check for uninvited guests who might want to share ???????????????

Printed in the United States
By Bookmasters